Network and Multi-Level Marketing Pro

The Best Network/Multilevel Marketer Guide for Building a Successful MLM Business on Social Media with Facebook! Learn the Secrets That the Leaders Use Today!

By Aaron Jackson

Table of Contents

Chapter 11: Why Some People Don't Make Money?

They Don't Have Enough Focus
They Do Not Have the Right Marketing Skills
They Lack Leadership Skills
They Did Not Have Enough Preparation
They Are Spending Too Much Time on the Wrong Activities
They Did Not Get a Good Mentor
They Did Not Have Good People Skills
They Did Not Go Out of Their Comfort Zone
They Were Too Concerned About Themselves
They Let Negative Influences Affect Them

Conclusion

Introduction

Congratulations on purchasing *Network and Multi-Level Marketing Pro: The Best Network/Multilevel Marketer Guide for Building a Successful MLM Business on Social Media with Facebook! Learn the Secrets That the Leaders Use Today!* and thank you for doing so.

The following chapters will discuss how and network marketing can turn your life around if you implement the right strategies. Do you dream of getting that dream house every day? Well, then here is the good news. With Network Marketing, your dream is going to come true earlier than you thought. With this book, you will learn all the secrets to Multi-Level Marketing that are used by the leaders.

If you are looking for an alternative to the age-old traditional pattern of upbringing and work, then this book is just what you need. There is no need to sacrifice the joys of this beautiful world in order to meet the demands of the corporate life. Although many people aspire to own a business, but it definitely takes a toll on you. It involves hours and hours of intense stress and the small to medium-sized business owners get very low returns on the investment made. Thus, after deducting the costs for staff, leasing, inventory, and operations, making profit becomes quite a struggle. The solution to all of this is Network Marketing as it will allow you to own your business the way you want to and at the same time, you do not have to do it all alone.

There are plenty of books on this subject on the market, thanks again for choosing this one! Every effort was made to ensure it is full of as much useful information as possible, please enjoy!

Chapter 1: All About Network Marketing and Multi-Level Marketing (MLM)

If you are into the business world, then you must have come across someone or the other using the term network marketing or multi-level marketing (MLM). This chapter will give you an introduction to the concept of both these terms and then we can proceed to the advanced topics.

What is the Difference Between Network Marketing and MLM?

The terms network marketing and MLM are often thought to be the same but they do have some subtle differences between them. You can say that they are two opposite sides of the same coin and so they are quite related but not entirely the same.

Let us start with MLM or multi-level marketing. This is a type of marketing where the business model is based on a referral program where people are referred to. The program itself also has been designed in such a way that it has several tiers. So, to make it a bit simpler, consider the following as an example. If I had referred someone into a particular MLM and that person, in turn, referred someone else, then you will be getting that other person's commissions as well with the help of your original referral.

On the other hand, network marketing is a type of business model which is all about distributors. The company will be implementing strategies to market their product to the various distributors in their niche. These distributors are a certain group of people who, in turn, are looking forward to setting up their own business and so they will be marketing the company's products in their way. For example, suppose a company is selling clothes but instead of devising a marketing policy for the general public, this company is marketing its products to distributors. The company will thus be preparing a marketing pitch for these distributors.

One of the best things about this is that it doesn't matter what the distributor does with the product. An initial sale is already being made by the company when they are selling their product to the distributor and the product is off their hands.

Should I Start Network Marketing or Build My Own Business from Scratch?

If you are pondering over whether you should start your own business or whether you should simply invest your time in network marketing, then let me tell you this. With network marketing, you do not have to take the hassles of marketing the product. You just have to come up with an excellent sales pitch so that you can show the prospect of your product to the distributors. Now, I would always suggest you to start network marketing and I can also provide you with some solid reasons to do so.

- Firstly, you must be thinking why you should start with network marketing. Well, to begin with, you do not have to stay stuck in any 9-to-5 job scenario. Thus, you can exercise a lot of freedom which any ordinary job will not be able to provide you with. After you have completed the initial steps, you will be able to conduct your marketing campaigns and literally run your own business right from your home. So, you will get to spend a lot of time with your family. Moreover, another great thing is that there is no income cap. If you are good at what you do, you can earn whatever amount you want to.

- You will not have to worry about any employees and thus, there is no hassle of hiring or firing anyone. And of course, you are not answerable to anyone. In short, you will be your own boss. But yes, you will have to maintain good relationships with the distributors and the agents but all of that doesn't involve you paying any wage to anyone and this in itself relieves you of so many responsibilities.
- There is an unbeatable amount of security in network marketing once you have finally set it up properly. Thus, no more worrying about becoming jobless or being fired by anyone.
- If for some reason, you are not able to stay on the clock, you do not have to worry about generating income as that will be taken care of on its own. If you assist others in setting up their business, you will always have your residual income.

But you always have to make sure that you are into a legit system and not some worthless pyramid scheme.

What Benefits Do I Gain from Network Marketing Companies?

In today's world, entrepreneurship that deals with network marketing are the fastest growing. There are so many benefits that you can enjoy with a network marketing model and here are some of them explained in detail.

No More Sky-High Startup Costs

Previously, when people used to think about beginning their own startup, they had to think twice about the costs and how they are going to fund it. But now with the advent of network marketing, you do not have to worry about the investment factor as there is almost no investment involved. Moreover, the little amount of investment that you will be making in this venture will be way less than your earning potential. So, if you think with clarity, you will see that your earnings will pay out much more than any other type of business. All that you will need, for example, marketing material, sales trackers, corporate training and so on are already in place with the operating systems of today.

Leverage

Network marketing involves a high amount of leverage and it promotes you to work smarter so that you do not have to put in a lot of effort and yet earn less. A day is made of only 24 hours and in that fixed amount of time, you have to do everything. You also need to spend time with your family and pursue your hobbies. If you are into a regular job, then you will be getting a fixed wage for, let's say, 8 hours a day. But in some cases, employees get paid based on the number of products they have sold. So, what I mean to say is that there is always a ceiling to the amount you can earn and with network marketing, you can break that ceiling. You will be making money while you are sleeping, traveling, or doing anything you want. All you have to do is slowly keep on increasing the number of distributors in your circle.

A Great Potential for Passive Residual Income

It's always better to have a back-up plan for the rainy days of your life. If your only back-up is your savings, then they are going to get depleted one day or the other. But with network marketing, you can pave the way for an ever-increasing scope of passive residual income. And to do this, you will need to master leveraging as already mentioned in the point above.

Amazing Tax Benefits

This is one of the perks of network marketing that people usually miss out on. Starting a network marketing company means you are doing it from your home. So, before you calculate the tax amount that you have to pay, you can deduct your expenses. If you are not aware of this, then the best solution would be to consult a tax specialist near you. He/she can guide you on what things you can deduct. One thing that you need to get straight is that your tax will always be calculated on the net income that you have after all the expenses have been deducted from it.

Freedom to Plan Your Own Day

When you are in a regular job, you are stuck in your cubicle for as long as your employer wants you to. You cannot come and go as you please. Your time is no longer yours because your employer is paying a wage for the time of day you are giving to his/her company. But in network marketing, you will be the master of your time. You can even choose with whom you want to work. You can go wherever you want and do whatever you want with your time and still make a sustainable income.

A Great Scope for Personal Development

If you are an employee in the corporate world, you will receive only that much amount of training which will make you capable of doing only that job. But you will get jailed within the walls of the corporate world. But in the case of network marketing, there are a lot of things that you will learn as you grow and this will lead to a lot of personal development. Why work for such long hours just to make someone else's dream come true when you can spend time with your family and build your own empire?

So, these were some of the benefits of pursuing network marketing. So, if you are thinking about starting your own network marketing business as well, then you need not worry at all because this book will guide you in a step-by-step manner towards your goal.

Chapter 2: Master Your Mindset Above All Else

You should not forget that network marketing, above all, is a business and so you should create a mindset where you treat it as a business. If you want to be a true leader right from Day 1, here are things that you need to in order to build the right mindset.

Envision Your Dream End Goal

To get success from your network marketing endeavor, having the right goals is necessary and you also need to visualize it each day. There is a scientific reason behind this as well. When you visualize what you want in life, your brain will get wired in a way that it will start identifying the resources that you need in order to achieve that end goal. Moreover, you will be creating an inner motivation that will be the driving force for you. When you think about the long run, envisioning your goals will also help you to stay on track by promoting positive thinking.

To ensure an efficient envisioning of your dream end goal, you first need to learn how you can assess your current situation perfectly. You first need to figure out where your contentment levels lie and then you can decide on what exactly do you want from your life. Your next step is to think about the dreams you have and the goals you want to fulfill. For this, you should sit in a calm place and make sure that you are not interrupted. You can either do this as the first thing you wake up in the morning because you will have more clarity and peace of mind or you can also do it at some other time of the day when you think the chances of interruption are low.

You must remember that your goals should be realistic. Don't set your goals so high that it becomes next to impossible for anyone to achieve them. Besides, you should also put a time frame to your goals as this will prevent you from becoming lethargic. You also need to make your goals specific. Some people set goals but they are too vague. You cannot simply say that you want to be successful in the next 5 years. You need to define what that success means to you. It can be something like – 'I will take my business to the next level and fetch 10% more profits in the next 2 years'. This is an example of a specific goal and this will prevent you from going off the track.

Spend 10 Minutes a Day Dreaming Your End Goal

Did you know that daydreaming about your end goals can actually make you successful? When practiced the right way, daydreaming might just end up to be the key to unlocking your potential. When you are dreaming about your goal, you are putting your thoughts into a perspective and this might just open new doors for you which you previously thought didn't exist. This can enhance your problem-solving skills as well.

When you imagine your goal in your head every day, you get to see various situations and you see the same thing from different perspectives. This will give you insight into your behavior in various situations that might occur in real life. But most importantly, dreaming about your goal even if it is for 10 minutes a day can make you happy and you will feel motivated to work even harder. When you are just starting out with network marketing and are skeptical about its success, dreaming about your goal will help you stay focused on what you want in life.

So, figuring out your goals is not the only step. You also need to dream about your goals because only then will you be inspired to give quantifiable effort to make those dreams turn into reality.

List 3 Things That You Want to Achieve and Achieve Them

You need to keep an eye on the progress you are making through your daily actions. Are they doing you any good? Well, to ensure that you get to enjoy the fruits of your actions, you can start nurturing a practice. We have already discussed in the previous points how goal setting is so important and so is dreaming. But if you are facing a problem in setting long-term goals or if you are not feeling motivated to fulfill what you are thinking then start with smaller goals.

List the small goals that need to be achieved first so that you can reach your ultimate goal. You can start by listing three goals at a time and then fixing a time span for them. For example, list 3 goals that you want to achieve this month and then devise the strategies and steps you need to follow to achieve them. You need to be determined to achieve those goals because the moment you do that, you will acquire a different level of confidence. You will get a feeling within yourself that yes, you can do it. And this feeling of confidence is very essential if you want to achieve bigger things in life.

These small goals will act as the road map to your success and by setting these small goals and achieving them one by one you will be taking baby steps towards your dream goal. Moreover, you will not be going around in circles. You will be following a definite path without remaining stuck in one position for a long time. The more goals you achieve, the more committed and inspired you will feel to stay on the path. The excitement of achievement will motivate and propel you to move forward and not look back.

Give Yourself a Pep Talk

Whenever someone says something motivational, it is bound to push your self-esteem levels higher. This will make you confident about whatever you were planning to do. But what if you do not have anyone in front of you who can give you that pep talk? Or maybe only you know the thing that you want to hear which will raise your bar of confidence. Then the solution is very simple indeed. You have to take the matters into your own hands and give yourself a pep talk. So, let's discuss how you can do it.

Did you do that exercise in your school where you had to rephrase the same sentence more positively? I'm sure you did but even if you didn't, this is something similar that you are going to do here. You need to strictly focus on keeping the language positive. For example, if you tell yourself 'Don't procrastinate', then there is a negative vibe about it. So, what you can say is 'You will complete all your tasks now so that you can have a lot of time in your hand later.' This sounds so much more positive, right?

Third-person self-talk or referring to yourself by your name or 'you' will often benefit you more. Moreover, it does not require much brainpower and is not taxing. Take deep breaths before you give yourself a pep talk because this will calm you down and you will be able to think more clearly. Now, you need not get too confused about what you are going to say. All you need to say are those words that you want someone else to say to you if they were the ones giving you a motivational boost. Or, you can think of it in another way as well. If your friend was in your shoes, what pep talk would you have given him/her? Say those same words to yourself.

Hold Yourself Accountable

Accountability is truly something that you need to master as it is one of the most valuable assets you have. If you are focusing yourself to grow both professionally and personally, holding yourself accountable is something that will take you far. Normally people think of accountability as a concept where you are answerable to someone else for your actions. But today we are not going to discuss any of that. Instead, you will learn why you should hold yourself accountable and not for someone else but you.

Think of it this way. Why should someone else be responsible for your success and failure when it is all about you? It shouldn't be anyone else's job to ensure that you are doing everything right, is it? If you do not hold yourself accountable for the things you do in life, you will never be able to achieve your goals or create a mindset required for network marketing. You might be having the best and most unique ideas about setting up your business, but would you be having a business if you do not put your ideas into action? No, right? So, it is of utmost importance that you hold yourself accountable because that will keep you striving towards achieving your goal.

You will notice that the moment you hold yourself accountable, you will be making steady progress. One of the biggest things about practicing accountability is that you have to set deadlines for everything and then make sure that you keep those deadlines. Setting a schedule is of paramount importance as you will know that you have a game plan set that you just need to follow. You also need to stop self-sabotaging yourself and practice positive accountability. Holding yourself accountable does not mean that you have to undermine your actions.

Pay Attention to Your Thoughts

If you want to truly understand yourself, then you have to start paying attention to your thoughts. What you see around you or what happens in your life is a direct result of your thoughts and so it is important for you to know what type of thoughts you are having. Your thoughts can cloud your judgment and they can also help you to think with clarity. They are the true indicator of your beliefs. You also need to check whether you are having negative thoughts. Positive thoughts will help in your progress whereas negative thoughts will only tie you down.

But if you detect any negative thoughts, you should never beat yourself up for that. The harsher you are on yourself, the more your negative thoughts will thrive. What you need to do is whenever you find a negative thought cropping up in your mind, write it down in your journal and then try tracing the root of that thought. Once you find the reason which led to that negative thought, all you need to do is replace it with a positive thought. You need to understand that positive thoughts are highly powerful and a single thought in the positive direction can bring down negative thoughts of 10 times its magnitude.

When you take the negative thoughts away, you prevent them from shaping your reality. Instead, you are promoting positive thoughts and that is how your reality will be. You need to visualize those positive thoughts because that will make them feel more real and vivid as if they are right in from of your eyes. This will increase the chances of them coming true and this will also keep you motivated to work towards a positive end goal.

Build an Inspiring Team of People

If you have ever worked as a part of a highly inspiring and motivated team, then you'll know what I am talking about. The pace of the members in your team becomes your pace as well and so you need to pick people who are highly energized. Of course, if you are just starting out, you can do everything by yourself. In that case, you need to surround yourself with people outside your work who will keep inspiring you and pushing you in a positive direction. You need people in your life who can give you the pep talk you so need.

But if you want to grow further and say build a six or seven-figure business, then you will have to recruit some people. Make sure you don't recruit random people into your business. The people you recruit should be truly motivated to work for your company. You need to become a positive leader yourself if you want to have a positive team. Identify the roadblocks and see if there are any aspects that can cause dissatisfaction among your team members. Try to eliminate these roadblocks in the best way possible. Create a healthy workplace environment.

Using a team charter will also keep everyone motivated. The charter will state what the role of each person on your team is. You should strive to create a nonjudgmental environment. Those who are working with you should not feel hesitation in voicing their opinions. If you want to build trust, then creating transparent relationships is the first step. All of this will together contribute to forming an inspiring team of people.

Stay Curious

Everyone has heard the saying *curiosity killed the cat*. But is it true? Well, it depends on the situation and in network marketing, you need to stay a little bit curious if you want to stay ahead of others in the game. The more curious you are, the more your listeners will feel that you are genuinely interested. Network marketing is all about relationship building and so staying curious will benefit you in several ways.

Are you looking for the potential target market for your products or reliable distributors? Or are you researching what techniques other leaders are using to make their business successful? No matter what you are doing, there are some basic questions which you should ask. These questions should revolve around the interests, goals, motivation, and the core values of the person in front of you. There is no end to the questions you can ask and these were only a few things to get you started.

The moment you start implementing curiosity as a part of your business culture, you will start getting some amazing results. When you are curious, you are literally hunting for newer and better answers with the same mundane questions. This can lead you to find some breakthrough ideas. This can open new doors for you which you never thought would. Thus, propelling your business to the next step will become a lot easier. Out of the box thinking is only possible when you are curious and with such an immense amount of competition in the market, if you want to stay in the game, you need to do something that no one else is doing.

You also need to think about some powerful questions because they can unearth some incredible ideas. And do you know what the best part is? Asking questions is completely free of cost. When you are curious, it shows how passionate you are about what you are doing. This is reflected in everything you do and both your customers and distributors and also your team members will be able to see it. Thus, curiosity will make you a true entrepreneur.

Chapter 3: Choosing the Right Company for You

There are already thousands of network marketing companies in the market and with each passing moment, several others are popping up. But if you want to get success out of your venture, choosing the right network marketing company is crucial. In the past, when the internet was not so well-developed and people did not have access to so much knowledge on a personal level, it was usually friends, relatives or some co-worker who used to introduce people to some network marketing company. But in most cases, such companies did not turn out to be good and led to modern success or in the worst case, failure. But today, you can do your own research to make sure that you do not end up with the wrong company. Here are some steps that you can follow to choose the right company for you.

Choose Your Niche and Discover Companies

One of the very first steps in choosing the right network marketing company is to figure out your niche. This might seem easy but can be really confusing so here is a step-by-step process that you can follow to choose your niche.

- **Evaluate your skills and strengths** – Everyone is good at something and has a particular passion. This is the first piece of your puzzle. You need to review what skills you have. For this, you can first think about the jobs that you have done in the past if any. This will help you write down the skills that you have acquired in your career. If you have not done a job in the past, then think about your passion and what skills you already have. Write all of this down and you will be noticing some common threads. This will help you narrow down your search. Don't just consider a niche because you love it. You should love it enough to genuinely have a passion for it and sustain yourself for at least 5 years in the same niche.

- **Research about the market for your niche** – Not every niche has a profitable market. So, when you are deciding on a niche, you need to make sure that there is a demand for that particular product or service. You can implement the keyword search method to do this. Use some relevant keywords in your niche and start searching on Google. Gradually, you can narrow the results by competition level, monthly search volume, and other parameters. In the case of the search volume, you should remain in the range of 1,000-10,000 per month. Anything less than 1,000 would suggest that the niche probably doesn't have that much market.

- **Check out the competition** – As already mentioned earlier, keyword research plays a very important role while you are choosing your niche but finding out about the competition is equally important as well. Select some keywords and then search on Google. You need to check the first page results of Google and which websites are ranking there. You will find a lot of well-known sites there. What you need to see is whether that niche is oversaturated or not. If it is already packed with other good sites, then it is always advisable to find some other niche. There can be another scenario as well. You might find no websites that rank for the keywords you have used. Yes, you might be thinking that this is a great opportunity for you but you need to keep in mind that this could also mean that others who had ventured into this niche prior to you have already discovered that the niche does not hold any potential. The best scenario is when you find a handful of sites in the niche but none of them are great. That is your cue to take the niche as the competition won't be tough.

Once you have selected your niche, now it is time for you to look at the companies that are present in this niche.

Consider the Stability and Longevity of the Company

Yes, it is indeed your efforts that can bring you success but at the end of the day, when you have invested multiple heads and have built a huge group, it is sensible to work with a company that will be present even after you have achieved all of that. The first thing to consider about the company you are planning to choose is its financial stability. For this, you should choose a company which has been around for at least 5 years. This will ensure that all the efforts that you have put into group building are not wasted. In the past couple of years, there have been so many network marketing companies that have come and gone.

The more the company has stayed in the market, the more experience they have. If the company has sustained itself for 5 years, then you can stay assured that it is here to stay. Most companies that go out of the market do so within the first five years of starting the business. Now, you definitely wouldn't want to find yourself to be a part of a company that doesn't have the stability, would you?

Learn About the Compensation Plan

The compensation plan is one of those factors of a network marketing company that will differ from one company to the other. You need to check what the compensation plan for this company is because if you are going to work with them, you also need to be comfortable with the compensation they are promising you. This factor is also important from the point of view that it is the one thing that will determine how quickly you are going to make money through MLM or network marketing. So, here are some points that I have specially jotted down for you so that you can evaluate the compensation plans more efficiently.

- **Be careful about companies flushing the sales volume** – There are some companies that do this. In the beginning, you will not be having any sales volume and so you might feel that this is not going to affect you. But later on, if you fail to reach the next threshold of sales volume, then you will have to begin at zero all over again. How frustrating is that! You might even fall for the temptation of ordering an extra product because you know that if you don't, you will not be able to reach the threshold. This will not bring you any significant money as well. So, always choose a company which doesn't flush the points. In fact, your next pay period will simply carry on the excess volume.
- **Avoid companies which limit the sales volume by depth** – When you are a beginner, level 1 people are those whom you first introduce. Then comes level 2, that is, the ones level 1 people introduce in turn. But when a business has attained a certain point in its growth curve, it will have tens and thousands of levels. But in several compensation plans, you might notice that the sales volume accumulation is limited to, say, only 5 levels deep. Keep in mind that 5 levels are pretty basic. Now, you might be

arguing the fact that 5 levels are a lot for you but you need to remind yourself that after a certain period of time, that same 5 levels depth will be nothing. In the long-term, you won't be paid anything for levels deeper than 5 and this is a huge loss.

- **The plan should be easy to understand** – Don't go for any compensation plan which is so complex that it becomes next to impossible for you to figure out how the compensation is being calculated. Whenever a plan is complex, it will come with a lot of rules and most of them will favor the company and not the associate. Moreover, it will not be easy for you to figure out whether you are receiving the right amount of compensation or not. Besides, imagine yourself trying to explain the same compensation plan to others? You wouldn't be able to do that unless you understand it yourself and so you will not have many people joining your network as well.

- **Check the frequency** – You will find many plans that have a monthly payment cycle. But when you opt for better plans, you can even grab the opportunity of getting paid weekly and in some cases, daily as well.

Pay Attention to the Specific Team You Are Joining

When you are deciding to join a specific network marketing company, you obviously need to have some knowledge about its team. Who are these people? Are their views in line with yours? How much experience do they have? Knowing all of this is of utmost importance. You should strive to be different and not just any other random recruiter. Be a leader. And for that, you cannot simply read the brochure and listen to the sales pitch and think, oh! I am done because no, you are not. You have to put in some effort and get off your couch to do some real work. Attend the events that are conducted by this company and you'll start gathering some image about its leaders.

Don't get railroaded just because someone gave you an amazing sales pitch. You need to do your own homework if you want to climb the ladder of success. No matter how much time it takes you to do the initial research, take your time because this research will be your foundation and you can't afford to get it wrong.

Determine If the Business Fits with Your Goals

If you are going to work with the company, then your ideals should be in alignment with the vision of the company as well. Everyone has some goals in their minds when they start out and so will you. Determine what those goals are and write them down. Then see whether this company is meeting your goals or not. If you simply enter a company on a whim and then you find out that the company is not keeping up to your expectations, then you will end up wasting your time and you will be dissatisfied as well. The more aligned your goals are with the company, the familial you will feel with the entire atmosphere.

In simpler terms, if the organizational goals and your personal goals are not aligned, you will be at quite a disadvantage. You will feel lost and it is very easy for you to become disengaged when your goals are not meeting. You will not feel connected with the rest of the team and everything will seem like a mess. So, it is important for you to determine this point right at the beginning.

Making the Final Pick of Which Company You Choose

So, now that you have gone through all the steps, it is time for you to finally make the choice. Now, here is a word of warning for you. Some people don't end up making a choice for a long time not because they are still researching but because they are procrastinating. You shouldn't be doing something like that. Procrastination in this case usually results due to the fear of the unknown but if you have followed all of the above steps carefully, you need not fear anything. Moreover, if you do not take risks in life, you will never be able to achieve anything big. Don't let fear brew inside your mind just because you got influenced by the opinion of others.

One of the key points that you have to keep in mind is that you can only become successful in your network marketing venture if you are passionate about it. You cannot excel in anything that you are doing forcefully. You will face different types of network marketing companies in the market but it is paramount that you go with the one that excites you and that you know you will be passionate to work with. While you are doing the research, you should also try and note down any of the key points that you love about a certain company. You should also note down the bad points or the challenging aspects. This will make it easier for you to narrow down the options at hand.

Another important thing that you have to keep in mind is the source from which you are taking all this information. Your source should be credible. Far too often people depend on opinions from those who have zero knowledge in this industry. Yes, some people are quite opinionated about this industry although they have zero knowledge about it. So, it is always advisable that you seek someone who has already got themselves established in this field as they can be a great mentor to you. So, when you are seeking the information, think twice and ask yourself whether the source is reliable enough. Is the source entrepreneurial? Are they financially stable or are they still struggling themselves?

You might be thinking why take all the hassle of approaching someone when I can simply use the Internet. Well, here is the thing – on the Internet, literally anyone can post anything and you wouldn't know how credible that source is. So, even if you are using the Internet for research and you come across some skeptical information, make sure you double-check it from somewhere else. If you keep all the nonsense of the Internet aside, it can provide you with some really valuable information as well and that too for free. But at the end of the day, you need to 100% sure that your final decision is not influenced by someone unqualified.

If you are still in a dilemma as to whether you should make the final choice or not just because you fear that you might fail, then know this – everyone's journey in network marketing is different. Just because someone you know has failed in his/her journey doesn't mean you will as well. Some people join network marketing with some prior knowledge on the same and thus they attain success way before than others. But that does not necessarily have to be you. Even if you entered this world with little or no skills, you will get success if you keep trying and implementing the right strategies and all of that starts with choosing the right company.

So, I'm sure by now you have some eligible companies on your list. There is one last thing that you have to do and that is you need to check online whether these companies have any complaints registered against their name. In case you find that one of the companies on your list has a complaint, strike that name off because why take the risk when you have so many other companies to choose from? So, start your research today and take your first step by choosing the network marketing company you want to work with.

Chapter 4: Making A Commitment to Growth

Commitment is an important key to reaching the end goal in network marketing. If you give up when the going gets tough, then you are not going to last long. You have to keep faith in your abilities and not end up becoming lazy midway. If you remain focused and committed, success will definitely come to you. If you are a new marketer, then it is very easy to become overwhelmed because of such a vast amount of information that is being thrown at you all at the same time. And in between all that, you might even think of giving up. But that is why I have created this chapter for every marketer out there so that you can learn how commitment plays a key role in growth and how you can master it.

Learn to See the Good in Things

Take some time out in your daily schedule and think about all those thoughts that go around in your head. Do you have thoughts that make you feel negative? Do you keep thinking that 'I'm not good enough'? Do these negative thoughts keep playing in a loop? Well, if the answer to these questions is yes, then you it is time that you learn how to see the good in things. If you don't then these thoughts will slowly chip away your belief in your own self and your abilities.

You might treat these negative thoughts like that of a gospel in your mind. In your mind, you might be thinking that it is realistic for you to know what you can do and what you cannot do. But have you ever asked yourself how you came to know these so-called facts in the first place? The answer is probably that you had told yourself the same exact things and now you treat them to be the truth. So, how can you be so sure that these negative things are in fact true? There is a term for these thoughts and they are called self-limiting beliefs. These beliefs are present in everyone in some way or the other and their presence is what keeps you restrained and you are not able to reach your goals.

You need to learn how you can see the good in things, in simpler terms, you need to be optimistic. You also need to understand the fact that you will not become a master of network marketing in a night. It will require time and practice. In the beginning, there will be struggles like any other journey but you have to remain on your track. If you face failure, embrace it, and learn from your mistakes. Treat every failure as your chance to learn and don't be too harsh on yourself because you are giving the best you can.

Commit to Working Hard Towards the Success

Everyone wants to stay committed to network marketing and everyone thinks that they have already committed every ounce of their energy to it but have you ever asked yourself – 'how committed am I?" Sadly, most people just know that they are committed but in reality, they aren't. They aren't ready to sweat it off to achieve success in network marketing. Most people don't even learn the basics properly and that is what gets them into trouble. But you have to be passionate about this if you really want to stay committed.

I cannot stress it enough as to the importance of setting an end goal and sticking to it. But keep in mind that your targets leading up to this end goal have to be realistic. In order to ensure that you stay committed to your goal, you need to check on yourself regularly as to how much progress you have made. Once you see the progress, make new goals if the situation requires you to. Now that you have clear goals, you also need to make the best use of your strengths and skills. If you really want to reach success and get better outcomes, then you need to start applying your skills to your day-to-day work scenes.

You also have to be honest with yourself. Assess yourself carefully and find out which are the regions where you are struggling with your network marketing skills. Self-reflection and then gradual improvement are the two things that you should consistently maintain in your day-to-day life. Remember that an inquisitive mind is what helps people move forward so if you have any questions, don't hesitate to ask them. But you need to ask them to people who are established in the field of network marketing. Doing all of this doesn't mean that you are not going to make mistakes. You will meet obstacles and occasionally, you might even fall down. But what is important is that you need to acknowledge your mistakes and get up again. That is what shows how committed you are to reaching your end goal.

Continue Approaching Growth with Consistency and Passion

Persistence and consistency are the two most important qualities that will help you make progress in life. And both of these qualities are possible only when you have the passion for what you are doing. But if not engaged on a regular basis, these qualities can be difficult to sustain. I do not have any doubt about the fact that you already know what benefits consistency can lend you in life. No matter what accomplishment you want to have in life, consistency is the key to it. According to the definition of the term, trying to bring out a favorable outcome in a chosen field by developing a discipline is called consistency.

If you implement a concerted effort to maintain an enduring focus, then you are bound to be rewarded with success after a certain point of time. There is a scientific basis for this as well. When you are trying to achieve something by focusing all your attention on your goals, your brain is also stimulated to lock its focus on the target. Whenever someone wants a favorable outcome, it becomes essential that you make your determination ceaseless. When people master the art of consistency, they automatically develop an inner drive that is unyielding. They also have a sharpened mind and they start developing their character too.

Those who are successful in becoming consistent with their approach towards growth know how to invoke positive results and they are not willing to make any compromises by relying on the road less traveled or cutting corners. And since network marketing is more like a task-oriented goal, staying consistent is the key as it will help you in tracking your results right up to completion. And you need to keep one thing in mind that when you are just starting out grasping the concept of network marketing, you might not be able to see any results prominently visible in front of your eyes. But if you are doing everything right, the results are probably being laid down as the foundation of your business. All you need to do is be patient and you will get to experience full-blown success.

Respect Yourself and Your Needs

Self-love and self-respect are not only essential for leading a happy life but also a successful one. And the most important part is that they apply to network marketing as well. There comes a point in everyone's life when outside influences tend to take your self-respect away from you but at that moment, you have to stand strong and resist that from happening. As you must have already understood, network marketing is all about building your network and thus engaging others. So, whenever we are talking about human contact, respect becomes a crucial aspect of it.

But you cannot really expect someone else to treat you with respect if you do not respect yourself in the first place. So, stop treating yourself like crap and start considering yourself worthy of everything. You will instantly notice how big of a difference it is going to make. So, you need to think about your needs and in network marketing, this means that you should not compromise on anything or settle for anything less than what you want.

You need to accept yourself and for once fight for what you want. If you want a certain amount of compensation rate, don't settle for something lower than that. If you think you need a few days off, just go ahead and take it. If you do not do the things that make you happy, you will not feel motivated to work towards your success. Moreover, if you spend your days just by trying to impress others, you will never be able to live for yourself. Build strong beliefs but also accept changes. Whatever you do, stand for yourself in every situation that comes your way.

Focus on Expanding in Every Way That You Can

For every network marketer out there, expanding your business should be among the top things to do in your priority list. You need to capture the benefits of network marketing and then use them as leverage if you truly want to expand. But first, you need to build your mindset in such a way that you are willing to do whatever it takes to expand. If you have a fear of talking to people, then you need to be able to break out of that shell. Similarly, if you have any other such insecurities, you need to deal with them one by one.

Your next task is to develop your entrepreneurial mindset so that you can effectively start recruiting people into your network. Don't ever be apologetic about approaching someone. You need to be bold and confident. You also need to know how you can increase your friend circle in the world of network marketing. Share hobbies with the people who are already established here so that you can increase your contact with them. But making friends doesn't necessarily mean you have to recruit them all. It simply means that you get more and more people to interact with and share your knowledge on this subject. If you are finding it difficult to do this, then promise yourself about interacting with at least one or two people in a day and this way, it will become a daily habit for you.

Always stay prepared for your pitch. Keep videos or articles explaining your business ready and keep them handy so that you can produce them whenever you see the time is right. You also need to brush up on your storytelling quality if you want to be a good network marketer. The more impactful and encouraging your story is, the more the number of people you get on board. You should be energetic, vibrant, and always enthusiastic because why should people work with you if you are not excited about your own venture?

Be Willing to Seek and Accept Feedback from Others

No one is perfect and no matter how well you are doing in your business, you will need to learn to face criticism because it is unavoidable. That moment when someone gives some negative feedback about your work is one of the toughest things to deal with. It definitely is not anyone's favorite activity. But you will lose out on a lot of lessons if you start avoiding these feedbacks because some of them can really help you improve. So, what is the solution? You have to learn how you can accept feedback from others. When received in the right way, you will see for yourself how different the outcome of feedback becomes.

When you hear someone else telling you that you were wrong or what you did was wrong, it definitely is a hard time for you. That criticism starts sounding like a threat to you and your brain tries to avoid it completely. Another important thing that psychology states about criticism is that our brain is programmed in a way that it often twists criticisms rather than changing its way of thinking. So, you never really remember what exactly the criticism was. You only remember what you deciphered it to be.

So, how can you learn to accept feedback? There are two important qualities that will help you in accepting feedback and they are – self-efficacy and self-esteem. These two qualities can change your behavior towards feedback. You need to be comfortable with both your limitations and your talents. Only then can you make improvements in your life in an easier manner. But what you are struggling with low self-efficacy and self-esteem? Well, the only way to solve the problem is to start setting micro-goals and then achieve them so that you can make a small amount of progress every day. You need to cultivate a mindset that is growth-based and then you will start noticing feedback in the light of improvement.

Commit to Learning About Your Business and Industry

If you had made a decision of starting your own business and then entered the world of network marketing, then you need to get one thing straight – your network marketing business requires the same amount of commitment as that of any traditional business. People often succumb to the thought that their business isn't reaping the results they wanted or the results aren't coming as quickly as they wanted it to come. But you need to commit yourself to learning more about your business and your industry if you want to be successful here. Every business runs in its own way and if you want to master it, you need to learn it.

You need to expose yourself to the various terminologies used in network marketing because this is the first step. If you are not aware of the terms used, how will you be conversing with others? You also need to ask if something is unclear to you. There is no embarrassment in asking and the only cowards are those who step back from asking.

Think of it this way – how does a doctor make money? He makes money by selling his knowledge in the form of prescribing medicines to his/her patients. You are doing the same thing in your own way. You have to use your knowledge in order to make profits. But first, you need to gain that knowledge and you need to be committed about learning it. No matter what your financial position is, your skills and knowledge will always play an important role. You can gain knowledge in whichever way you deem fit. You can take courses or you can even self-educate. The choice is yours. Moreover, you can also approach someone to mentor you.

So, these were some of the ways in which you can build your commitment in network marketing. Step out of your comfort zone and make the necessary changes and you will see yourself moving towards your goal. It is normal to have fear but don't let your fears control you or hold you back from expanding your business because then, you will be the only one to lose anything.

Chapter 5: Promoting Your Products and Events

The network marketing business is all about the products and so promoting them is crucial if you want to make some profit. Consequently, holding events and promoting them is equally important because that will help you build stronger relationships. These events can also be used as the place where you educate others about your product and why they should choose it. At its core, network marketing is all about building relationships and maintaining effective communication. So, follow the tips mentioned below and promote your products and events.

Build a Brand for Yourself

The competition in the space of network marketing or MLM is rising every single day and so what you bring to this market should be unique. And what else is more unique than your own personality! Thus, it is always advised to brand yourself. And to do this, one thing that you have to make sure is that all your social media platforms are centered around you and they carry your image and name. If you want to be surefooted about your stand in the market, then you need to make yourself the brand. You don't want to be remembered as the 'person who sells the X product', right? You should be remembered by your name and for that, you have to build a brand for yourself.

It is not that hard as you imagine it to be. You have to go ahead in a step-by-step manner and you will definitely succeed at it. In order to do the branding properly, use your own products proudly and no matter what conversation you are having, refer to your brand and products. If you consider embodying the company brand as a strategy for business growth then others (mostly your potential leads) will start understanding your worth and know that you are the real deal here. One of the first things that you need to ensure is to keep your word. If you decide or say that you are going to do something, then follow it to the end.

Companies will come and go but you need to remind yourself that you are here for the long haul and you are going to remain here even after the companies have all gone. Everyone has a starting point and so it doesn't matter that you are starting from ground zero. It is never too late to take the first step. You need to decide on the brand direction first. Put all your focus on building a loyal customer base so that you can be sure that you always have a group of customers who are genuinely interested in your brand.

You also need to figure out what you enjoy the most. If you are confused with this part, just ask yourself, what would you not regret making content about even after 10 years from now? If you are taking this business seriously, that means you have to think long-term and there is no use picking something about which you will quickly lose all your interest. People always prefer those who are confident and when you choose something you love; you will automatically feel confident while speaking about it.

Take Advantage of Video Marketing

When it comes to the promotional toolbox, video marketing is definitely a very powerful arsenal mostly because it can impact your audience deeply. Videos are more memorable than any other form of content and they are highly engaging as well. They can establish a deeper and more emotional connection with your audience and you need to take full advantage of it. Are you confused about getting started? Then here are some ways that you can implement.

- **Introduce yourself** – This is the first and foremost thing that you need to do. You definitely need to have an introductory video because that will explain to your audience who you are, what products you sell and what value you can add. Moreover, with a video, you can easily impart your personality to your brand. But you should also think about the personality that you should portray. Of course, staying natural is good but you also need to think about it from the business point of view. Figure out who your target audience is and then find out what kind of personality would they love to see.
- **Share details about your business** – It has been seen that people are always attracted to videos that are explanatory. So, when you are giving the introduction, it is natural for people to become interested in your business but you have to grab their attention and keep them seated till the end of the video. You can even portray how the products can be implemented in real life or you can also show some behind the scenes work at your office.
- **Don't forget the customer testimonials** – When your audience will see happy customers saying good things about your products, it would automatically leave a positive impact on the minds of the audience. Moreover, this will benefit your SEO in spreading a positive word about your business. Another thing is when people notice that you have taken the time to collect feedback from your existing customers it means that you care for them. Thus, you are giving a very strong social proof about the quality of your products and people's trust in your brand.
- **Answer questions** – Your audience might have some questions about your business or products so make an FAQ-style video where you can answer the commonly

asked questions. Or, you can also ask your audience on social media about the questions they have and then answer all of them through a video. This will help you in generating loyal customers.

Create Content Specifically for Your Ideal Client

The kind of content that you are creating plays a huge role in attracting potential customers. If you are in this world of internet marketing, then at one point or the other, you must have heard of the phrase – 'content is king' and it truly is! While this might seem simple to you now, there is a lot of work that goes on in the background. Moreover, creating content for your ideal client is a very crucial part of SEO strategy. That is why you need to have all knowledge about your clients as missing out on the details would mean content of sub-par quality as well.

There is a myth that plagues the world of network marketing and that myth says – content is for advertising. Well, the picture might be somewhat like that but the main aim of the content is to educate and keep your audience engage. In most cases, when people practice a direct selling attitude in their content, the audience does not prefer such content. Your content should be able to interest your client and it should also have the ability to help you form a relationship with your client. Every piece of content should add some value and you should be planning for the content way ahead.

You need to understand that not everything is about you. You should try to put forward your personality but that doesn't mean that the content has to be about you. When you make the content about you, no matter how good it is, it might not generate any leads. Of course, you can speak about the achievements in your personal life so that your audience sees you as the leader but you should never dwell on your own achievements. Your content should be focusing on addressing the needs of your customers and something that will make them want to share your content on social media.

You should have a clear and detailed picture of your audience fixed in your mind. You also have to figure out the aim of your content and what outcomes do you want. Once you have done both of the things, you will find that brainstorming newer ideas becomes way easier. You need to think like your audience to come up with content that will appeal to them. The essence of creating a long-term marketing strategy is to always place yourself in the shoes of your customer.

Attend Events That Your Audience Would Attend

One of the key strategies of network marketing is for you to attend more and more events. You should select these events on the basis of your audience. You need to go to those events where your audience is going as well. Stop adopting the approach that everyone else is using. Build your own path. Going to events will help you in market research. You will not only learn about the efforts that you are competitors are making but you will also learn what other like-minded individuals have to say. If you think that market research is something that can be done only in the initial phase of your network marketing, then you are wrong. Market research is an ongoing process and you should never stop doing it even if you have attained a certain level.

When you attend events specific to your niche and your audience, you will stay in the know-how of recent events. This will prevent you from running towards something that is already outdated in this industry. You will learn the things that your audience thinks are important and so the roadmap to your goal will be charted out. The networking part of network marketing is of huge importance but beginners often forget that you also have to build a network outside of your own environment.

When you attend events in your industry, you will meet so many people and you might even start getting some new ideas after talking to those who are already in this industry. You will also meet some influential people and above all, your audience.

When you confine yourself within four walls of your office or home, getting new ideas may become a tad bit difficult. But when you go out and converse with others, you might get a fresh angle to something old and boring. Besides, when your audience is present at the same event, you will get a better insight into their problems and what exactly do they expect from the products. You will also get to see your audience up close and this will give you a better idea about who they are and with what strategies can you grab their attention.

Show the Products in Use

So, now you that you have figured out the basics of product and event promotion, I go back to the point I had mentioned once in the above paragraphs, that is, showing your products in use. Social proof acts like magic on your audience and they will instantly start having faith in your brand and your products. And if you are not aware of this then know that you can do so much more than just posting photos through social media. You can create a solid UGC or user-generated content campaign because it can leave quite an impact.

When people truly love your products, they will love to create videos or photos surrounding it. Whether they are simply chatting about your product or using them in a photo or video, there is no other greater authentic way to portray your product. This way, you can reach a way wider audience. Now, you might be wondering how can you get your customers to create such content. Well, the perfect way to do it is to simply ask for it. Facebook is an amazing platform to do this.

It has been seen that 62% of the customers prefer that the brand creates some content that demonstrates how they can actually implement the product in their day-to-day life. You can also start doing Facebook Live videos where you can answer the common questions asked by the audience, promote sales and also share some creative facts about your product. Another thing that you can do is use some UGC in your own videos thus, showing your audience how the existing users have used your product.

If you want to reach new customers who have the same likes and preferences as your current customers, then what you can do is work on improving customer referrals. If you have gained a considerable amount of followers on your social pages, then you can simply mail your customers for a small review if they liked your product and those who have genuinely loved it will not hesitate to give you a good review. Whenever you get a 5-star rating on your social pages, it can have an incredible effect on search engine results and automatically bring your page to the first page of Google search. No much how much effort it takes, having social proof of your products is definitely worth all the effort.

Don't Focus Entirely on Sales

You need to keep a lot of things in mind because the world of network marketing is all about the people and you have to deal with different types of people at the same time. There will be people of different interests and of different ages. So, before you start focusing entirely on the sales, you need to learn how you can relate to these people. The more you relate to them, the more you will understand their point of view. Of course, you need to maintain an individuality to stand out but too much of that can ruin your business as well. So, you need to become a bit more relatable by relinquishing some of that individuality.

When you are inviting others to have a look at your products and business, you should not try to sell something so much that the person in front of you becomes irritated. You need to remember that this is a two-way process. You can only sell to someone who is willing to buy. The stigma that is associated with the world of network marketing has happened due to a handful of people who are so annoying and they do not know that sometimes they just have to take a 'no' for an answer.

Make friends in the industry. You don't need to wake up every morning stressed with the fact that you have to make a new prospect today. Every random person you meet does not have a bull's eye on their forehead so you should not treat them like that. Instead, be friendly and be subtle when you are mentioning your business. You need to make your way of presentation interesting so that the person is genuinely interested in it. You have to produce some value and you will find people flocking towards you.

Do not practice aggressive strategies. Focus on your time and energy on quality. Moreover, you need to be confident about what you are selling as well because if you are not confident with your own product, why should others? And lastly, failure is a real thing but that doesn't mean you need to be afraid about it. Just go on with your plan and wait to see the results.

Chapter 6: Presenting Your Opportunity to Prospects

There is a term that is widely used in the world of network marketing and this term is called – 'prospecting'. It is the process of figuring out who are the potential people who might have some interest in your business. When it comes to network marketing, these potential people might either want to buy a product from you or might have some interest in joining your business. This chapter is going to focus on how you can present your opportunity to your prospects and make them interested in your business.

Inviting Them to Approach You

Start by making a list of your prospects. If you want to build a stable network marketing business then one of the important steps of it is to make a list of those people whom you know that you will be able to approach and invite. Then these people will come and have a look at your idea. This step has an important role to play yet most network marketers overlook its importance. Not giving this step enough importance might even give you a bad start recovering from which will take quite some time.

Another important tip for you when you are making this list of prospects – never think about who might be interested in hearing you out and who won't. This is because you'll never know for sure if you do not discuss your business with them and striking off a name from the list might just lead you to lose a potential prospect. So, stop pre-judging people and start brainstorming some names right away. Okay, now that you have your list of prospects ready at hand, it's time for you to get to the second step. You have to call up these prospects and invite them over. You should state the invitation in a way that your endeavor will interest them as well.

There is no right or wrong way to approach and what works for someone else might not work for you but there is nothing wrong about trying. So, if you are working for a network marketing company, have a look at their prospecting methods and what approach did they use. Start implementing that approach in your methods as well and then keep on checking your progress from time to time. If you think that you are not being able to reach the results that you thought you would, it's time to reassess your ways and find the flaws. You can even go to your mentor because sometimes a small change is all you need and an expert eye can help you with that.

Don't expect things to start yielding results straightaway. When you take up something new, do you become an expert right from the first day? No, right? Similarly, for network marketing, you need to give it some time to sink in and once you are into the swing of things, everything will start falling into place.

You should also invite more people than you actually anticipate will show up. In short, if you want 30 people to attend your event or meeting, then you should invite at least 50 of them.

Let Them Ask You Questions

What your main aim should be when you are approaching your prospects is that your product should be able to pose the solution to the problems of your prospects. So, you need to understand what the needs of your prospects are. You should let them ask your questions. This is because when they start asking the questions, it will reveal a lot about what they want to achieve. Some of the common questions that your prospects can ask you are listed below –

- **Who is your target customer?** This is one of the common questions as every prospect would want to know whether your product will be beneficial to them. If your product doesn't align with the kind of customers the prospects deal with, there will be no profits for the prospect and thus they will back down from making any deal. When you give them a response to this question, they will be scanning your answer for any inconsistencies between the type of target customers they have and the type of buyer your product needs. That is exactly why the need to research your prospects before reaching out is essential. When your answer is to the point, your prospect will know that you have researched them well. Your answer should be satisfactory to let them know why they are the perfect clients. You have to make your prospects feel that your product is the perfect fit for them.
- **Do you use your own product?** Whether a network marketer uses his/her own product acts as a litmus test. This proves that you are not only talking about the advantages provided by the product but you also believe in them. You need to go out of those pre-written sales scripts and make your point. Your experience as first-hand use will often impress your prospects more. If you want to place a better impression, you can gather some testimonials of your customers and present them to the prospects.

Lead the Conversation Without Pressure

Stepping out of your comfort zone and conversing with others is the way you should proceed with network marketing. If you start doing this, you will see growth gradually. But you also need to be confident in your conversations and practice leading the conversations without showing any symptoms of being under pressure. Moreover, you have to sound like a natural and not start presenting yourself as a salesperson. You need to make the conversation about your product and your prospects. It should not be entirely about you. Have you ever heard anyone talking so much about themselves that the other person got bored? If you have, then you'll know what I am talking about. It almost seems that the person is simply talking to himself/herself and not to prospect.

Several factors impress the prospects and make the conversation great. Firstly, when you speak confidently, the person in front of you will take you seriously. You need to make your conversation engaging and interesting so that there is a perfect flow. When you are leading the conversation with confidence, you will notice how easy and free-flowing it is and it will move from one topic to the other organically without pushing too hard.

If you want to build a long-term relationship with your prospects where they are satisfied in working with you, clarifying their expectations forms a major part of it all. You need to ask your prospects how much do they expect to earn from the venture so that this is worth their time. This way of framing your question is way better than simply blurting out 'Will you love making $15000 a month?" You shouldn't set someone's goal for them. You should give them the freedom to choose it themselves. When you do this, your prospect will be choosing something they know that they can achieve. If you frame the goal then it might become too high and scare them off and on the contrary, if it is too low, your prospects might lose their interest altogether.

Ask them about how many hours they are willing to commit to the cause and how long do they think will be required for them to reach success if they keep working consistently. This will ensure that you are getting a long-term commitment from this person.

Subtly Create a Sense of Urgency

Even though your product is the perfect one for your prospect and you are offering some good discounts, there is one thing that you are missing out. You are not creating a sense of urgency. In order to do that, you need to ask the right questions and you have to make your prospect think that they are in a dissatisfactory situation with their business. When there is no urgency, people don't usually take any action. They start procrastinating and take a lifetime to reach any conclusion whatsoever. But when you create a situation where time is a sensitive parameter, your prospects will not delay their decisions. And you are going to do it by asking some questions.

- **Ask how their business is going on** – Ask them the size of their company at present in terms of various factors like approximate customer number, annual revenue, and employee headcount. Once you ask this question, you will get an idea about what the vision of your prospect is and what obstacles are standing in their way currently. You should also ask your prospect whether their business is flourishing or is it suffering from some setback. This will instantly remind the person in front of you that they have overarching business goals and that is your cue to make them believe what an important role your product will play in helping them out. You can also throw in some new information, for example, a new trend in the market, and ask your prospect whether they knew about this or not. You need to pick something that your prospect won't probably be aware of. On knowing this new piece of information, they will see you in a more credible light and want to act as soon as possible.

- **Ask about their pain points** – You need to know what pain points your prospect is experiencing and then you should ask them why they are seeking to resolve those pain points now. The response will give you knowledge about how much urgency the prospect is already facing. Ask your prospect about the effects of the problem on their revenue and other factors and whether the problem is affecting a lot of people or not. When the prospect answers this question, they will start to realize that the effects are quite widespread and they need to start doing something about it.

- **Ask about the competition** – You should ask about the amount of competition that your prospect is facing. As a matter of fact, most industries are getting competitive but when your prospect answers this question, it will dawn upon them that they need to act now so that they can get ahead of others. You can also ask them whether they have lost any big customer at any point of time or recently. If they say no, then you can appreciate it and then subtly say how bad it would be if 20% of the revenue just disappears all of a sudden if it happened to you. If they say yes, they have lost customers, you will come to know that your prospect is ready to take precautions so that they do not have to face any such issues later on. You should also enquire about the incident because when your prospect vocalizes that big a loss, they will become even more eager to avoid such a catastrophe in the future. Then, it will be your duty to show how your product can solve the problem.

Have a Resource Available for Them to Read Over

The underlying aim of prospecting will always be effective communication and finally winning over the prospect to your side. After you have spoken with the prospect, you should always keep some resources available either in physical format or digital so that your prospect can read it over. This will clear out any doubts that the prospect might be having about your business. There are several other benefits of keeping a resource available as well.

One of the major benefits is that the resource will be able to educate your prospect about your business in a detailed manner. Moreover, the written resource will act as a recap to what you have just explained to the prospect in words. You need to be very careful while framing this resource. You need to make it comprehensive because only then your prospect will understand that you have the competence to do what it takes to keep up with his requirements.

In simpler terms, the resource you frame has to be valuable to your prospect. It should be convincing but not too pushy. There is no standard length to compose it. All you have to do is make sure that you have covered all the important points in a composed format. Don't exaggerate or don't write too lengthy passages that the prospect finds it boring too read. Keep it engaging, simple and flowing. Keep the overall tone warm and make sure you convey everything you need to win over the prospect. Also, you can tweak the resources each time you meet a new prospect and make it personalized for him/her. If you do that, the prospect will understand that you are truly interested in working with them and that you have done your research.

Always Request to Follow Up

Following up is a crucial part of your network marketing business when you are inviting your prospects. But people often do it the wrong way and this mess up the number of sign-ups that you could have got. If you are thinking that your prospect will sign up with you right after the first meeting, then you are wrong because most of the time, they don't. A single exposure is usually not enough to make someone say yes. You will have to devote some time to educate your prospects and only then will they have a full understanding of the opportunity at hand.

You might have made an endless list of prospects and you might even have delivered the best presentation anyone could ever give, but does that mean you have won their trust? No! They will not be impressed until and unless you send follow-ups. This is what keeps the conversation going and also builds a base for your relationship to develop. After that, your prospects will take a decision. Firstly, you need to set a specific time and that too during your first meeting with the prospect. When that specific time is over, you are going to send your first follow-up. You cannot back up after a week and suddenly decide you are not going to send the follow-up because that only shows how professionally inefficient you are. Don't ever fall back on your word.

Follow-up is nothing but a second form of exposure after your first meeting with the prospect. The greater the number of exposures, the more your prospect will be inclined in taking the decision. You need to set it in your mind that the goal of sending out follow-ups is to educate your clients and not to pester them into signing up. If one follow-up doesn't help you out, you need to send follow-ups after follow-ups. You can talk about true stories where the lives of people have been changed after using your product. So, in this way, you will be fostering a relationship with your prospect.

Follow all the above-mentioned steps correctly and be consistent because excellence is acquired only if you continue to practice.

Chapter 7: Converting Prospects into Distributors or Customers

Now that you have learned the presentation part, the next step is to learn the art of converting your prospects into distributors or customers. The more the number of conversions, the more money you will make but more importantly, you will be practicing a smarter conversion strategy as well. So, here are some ways in which you can convert your prospects effectively.

Spend Time Getting to Know Your Prospect

The first step to improving your conversion rate is to improve your own skills. You need to spend some time knowing your prospect because that will give you a clear idea about where they are coming from and what type of approach will help you win them over. Everyone has some pain points which you can use in making your pitch. For example, one of your prospects might be a bit shaky about the entrepreneurial side of the entire network marketing business. So, you need to utilize it and get started there.

You will come across several people who are simply interested in being a customer and not a distributor. They might not be willing to take up such a responsibility right now. Your job is to not let them feel any less than the others. You need to give them equal importance and make them feel that it is totally okay with you even if they want to be associated with your products right now. Once they are involved with your product, keep in touch with them through your newsletter or your social media.

Once you build a connection with the customers and they start seeing the social proof of your products, they might be getting interested in being a distributor after a while. You have to wait for the correct opportunity and then bring up the matter again. Most people who do not agree to become a distributor right away do so because they are afraid that their knowledge is just not enough to excel. But it is always your job to educate them and make them feel confident about it. The more you know your prospect, the better strategies you can come up with in order to convert them.

Initiate the Conversation with a Question

One of the biggest struggles that any network marketer, who is new to all of this, faces is starting a conversation with the prospect. Once you go through this, you will get a better idea about the strategies you can implement. Well, for starters, you need to relax and stay confident. Your conversation should not sound sales talk or awkward. A mistake that everyone makes is they drag the conversation for too long. Don't! If you spend most of your time simply trying to build rapport, it might just have the opposite effect. No person would like the fact that you spend an hour talking only to state that you have some business ideas to share and that this was the point of the conversation all along.

You need to get to the point and you need to find some common ground between you and the prospect. It is usually advisable that you start the conversation with a question. All the standard ice breakers in the field of network marketing are all questions. The most common one is starting with something like – 'Do you aspire to have multiple streams of income?' Another common one is – 'Will you interested in making some side money if it doesn't mess with what you are already doing?' These are some age-old icebreakers and they continue to work even today but some people hesitate to start off with this right away. Don't worry I have got you covered as well.

One of the easiest ways to break the ice and start off a conversation with someone you just met is to engage in small talk but with motive. For example, you can notice the details in their appearance and compliment them about it. If you like what they are wearing, just tell them you like it and ask them where they got it from. Continue talking to the person and then eventually you will get to the point where you can get to ask what he/she does for a living. Learning about the occupation of the person in front of you gives you just the right opportunity to start talking about MLM and its scope.

You can go about it like 'I do a side business and this fetches me so and so income.' Start stating all the advantages of doing network marketing. Most people, after this point in the conversation, will become interested and ask you about further details. What you can do is you can give them your business card and maybe say, that you have a conference call to attend and you will keep in touch to tell them about the rest of the details. The excuse for the conference will help you break the communication and this is necessary because you should not give out too much information at once as it might scare off the person and break the sale. But don't forget to follow them up if you give them your business card and aim at getting some sign-ups!

Answer Any Questions Your Prospect Might Have

Do you get excited every time you are in a sales conversation? Well, everyone does. But the trick is to be able to close the deal and one of the key steps to that is answering the questions that your prospects ask in the right manner. An even better approach to answering the questions like a pro is to anticipate what questions they are going to ask and then keep all the resources and content you need ready at hand so that your answer sound professional and convincing. Some of the common questions that your prospect might have are listed below –

- **What makes you different from the others?** You should know that this is where you need to make yourself seem interesting and catch your prospect's attention. What makes you different from others is what will make the prospects come to you. You can talk about what makes your approach different. Focus on the skills that you have and you can also emphasize the message in the form of a written sales page that you can pass across to your prospect. On that page, you can keep a part titled 'Our Difference' and that is where you will explain what makes you different.

- **What can I expect if I sign up with you?** It is very natural for the prospects to want to know about your procedures and what methods you engage in once someone signs up with you. So, what you can do is, you can address this question right away in your conversation so that your prospect comes to know about it without even asking for it. But you also need to ensure that whatever you say will happen, actually does because this will lay a better foundation for your relationship with your prospect. You can also include a 'What to expect' portion in the resource file or sales page that you pass on to them.

- **If I sign up with you, how can you help us?** This is somewhat similar to the previous question. The only difference is that here the focus is more on the improvement that will occur and not only on the methods you use. You have to answer this question in a way that your prospect understands how much value you impart with your services. It should not be about selling your products but rather about the values. You can also give examples stating how the businesses of other prospects have improved after they signed up with you.

- **How much expertise do you have in this industry?** This too is a very common question because the prospects might want to know whether you have worked in their industry or not. This will directly reflect on the skills you own. That is why you need to have an 'Industries Served' section on your sales page. If you have a website then include this section there as well. Under this section, include some gripping and impactful case studies related to that particular industry.

- **What is your pricing?** Clarifying the budget is something you should do quite early in your conversation so that the prospect doesn't have to ask you this question at all. This also ensures that there is no waste of time and you can get to work right away. Many people prefer not to publicize their pricing but even if you do choose to publicize it, make sure you have varying levels of package offerings on your site. This will let the prospects know that if they want to engage with you, they can do so at different levels.

- **Can we get the contact of someone who has previously worked with you?** You will find this question cropping up with several clients as they tend to feel more comfortable once they have spoken with some of your clients. This brings to light the importance of maintaining happy clients. If you keep your clients happy, they will have only good things to say about you and this is going to benefit you a lot. But before you give the contact of a client to a prospect, make sure you have a word with the client first. And, you can always include client testimonials on your website for some added emphasis.

- **Who will be my primary contact?** Always remember that it is you who built the rapport with your client in order to bring him/her on board. So, if you suddenly say that you have set someone new to be their primary contact, they might not be too happy about this. So, that is why you need to discuss this at the beginning of your conversation where you can say how the entire work is looked after and who performs what role in your business.

Make Your Pitch

Now that you have gathered some knowledge, it is time for you to make the pitch! But you need to keep it short and simple. Don't make it too lengthy. But make sure you cover everything in a short span of time and you bring home the point you are trying to make. Don't ever use any jargon because that might only confuse your prospect. The best way to make the perfect pitch is to practice. You can write down what you have thought about and then you can practice it over and over again so that it all comes naturally to you and doesn't sound like you have memorized all of it just for the meeting.

While your words are of utmost importance in your pitch but so is your body language. You should not only sound confident but also look confident. Don't sound creepy or desperate, just be natural. Wear smart clothes and stand straight. Another thing that you should keep in mind is that your pitch should not sound monotonous. Your enthusiasm should be prominent because that will make the prospect realize that you really love what you do and you are happy with the results yourself.

Do you have a habit of speaking too fast? Then you have to do something about that as well. Practice beforehand until you master the art of speaking at the right pace. Any abnormality in your pace of speaking can make your words unclear and your prospect might end up misunderstanding your words or not understanding them at all. The bottom line to all of this is that your speech has to be good. It should be catchy and something that your prospects can easily remember.

When you are giving the initial speech, your aim should be identifying who is interested in doing business with you and who is not. You can leave the rest of the details for a later presentation where you can give a more explanatory speech. Making a complete presentation to someone who might not even be interested does not make sense.

Chapter 8: Creating A Strong Follow-Up System

When you start with network marketing, your primary focus is spreading the word so that you can attract new prospects. But producing your pitch in the most exciting way is not where you get the prospect on board. There is a lot more to do than that. Beginners in the world of network marketing often forget the fact that if they want to get prospects on board, they have to give them a considerable amount of time and in that time, they should prepare and educate them in a way that the prospect takes the decision to come on board without any second thoughts at all. And a follow-up system plays a very important part in all of this.

When to Use Automated Follow-Ups?

Having an automated system of follow-ups definitely saves a lot of time especially when you are busy with other aspects of the business. Here are some eye-opening statistics for you that will make you rethink about your follow-up strategy –

- Among the small business owners, 44% don't do more than one follow-up with their prospect
- 10% of the small business owners end up making more than three follow-ups
- Out of all the sales made in the network marketing world, 80% happen somewhere between the 5th and 12th follow-up

So, now you see the mistake here? A major percentage of businesses are actually missing out on their closing opportunities just because they are not engaging in an effective and consistent follow-up system. The problem with small businesses is that they have so much to do on their own that they don't get enough time for follow-ups. They always have to do something and so after trying a couple of times, they move on to the next task at hand. So, they don't have the patience or time to manually go through the entire process of tracking the emails that have been sent or track the leads. That is where the role of automated follow-ups come in.

With automated follow-ups, you will have your email campaigns ready at your disposal and these emails will be sent even while you are busy doing some other work. So, you need not take any stress about sending these emails at all. And if you are thinking that automation will make your emails stiff then you are wrong. With the new technology that is evolving, you can get your automated emails personalized as well. There are some prospects who require at least a twenty-time follow-up before they finally agree on joining and doing all those follow-ups manually can be quite cumbersome. So, an automated follow-up system will be your savior.

When to Use Manual Follow-Ups?

If a prospect is too important and you know that he/she can mean a lot to your business, then you can skip the process of automated follow-ups and do it manually. In this way, you can tweak the emails here and there and make it even more personalized. This will also make the prospect feel that you have done your research and you are really interested in having him/her on board. But this does not mean that you have to write all of the emails. You can create templates of your own and keep them handy for these situations. Then all you have to do is tweak these templates from time to time based on your prospect.

How to Create an Automated Follow-Up System?

Confused about how your automated follow-up system should look like? Don't worry this section has got you covered. I have demonstrated it in a step-by-step process so that you can accomplish the most with your automated system. It might take some time now but remember that the time you put into developing this system will ultimately bring you dividends every time you have a new prospect.

Step 1 – Start Afresh

The first step is to discard any old follow-up emails or strategies that you have because we are going to create everything from scratch. In this way, you can bring a fresh perspective. Remember that you might have the temptation to make changes to your existing system but that will only lead to minor incremental improvements and not anything significant. So, if you are aiming for a major leap in your performance levels then starting afresh is necessary.

Step 2 – Choose the Destination for the Follow-Up

This is the next most important step and it will also determine how your follow-up is going to be. You need to separate the follow-ups into two categories. One of them will be for your prospects and the other one for your prospects. Your customer won't simply walk up to you. You have to make him/her come to you by proper implementation of strategies, trust-building and educating. So, you need to envision the ideal experience that you think your prospects want and then you need to write down a summarized version of it. First of all, start with the experience that you want your prospects to have and then write the experience you want them to have as a customer.

Don't exaggerate the process too much and keep the descriptions crisp and short. Don't go overboard with anything. Remember that you are only picking the destination here and not making the plan. All you need to do is jot down a few important things that you aspire to have as a result of your follow-up marketing. You can think of it as your mission statement. When you have written down everything and you are satisfied that this is exactly what you want them to experience, it is time for you to move on to the next step.

Step 3 – Figure out What You Are Going to Do on the Way to Your Destination

You need to spend some time on this step and consider what exactly do you want your follow-up to do for you. Do you want it to increase your referrals? Or do you want to establish trust? There are so many things that you can aim to do and some of them are mentioned   below   –

- Increase social media following
- Increase repeat visits
- Shorten the buying cycle
- Reduce refunds
- Create reviews and testimonials
- Increase the frequency of orders
- Convert your customers into evangelists
- Position yourself as the best in the industry
- Increase engagement
- Give a full description of the product options that are available
- Develop a community
- Educate them on the overall industry
- Increase the frequency of orders and so on.

This is just an example of a wish list. Your goals can be anything. Don't think about what is feasible or realistic because that is going to limit your opportunities. Just write down all the ideas that you are having. Once that is done, you need to separate the goals into parts – pre-sale, that is, prospects and post-sale, that is, the customer. Then, arrange your goals in chronological order.

Step 4 – Figure out the 'How'

Now that you have figured out what you want from your follow-up emails, it is time for you to create a proper plan as to how you want to do it. For example, if you want to increase engagement, you can do so by incentivizing social media follows or write blog posts. This is where you have to brainstorm various ideas by which you can achieve your goals.

Step 5 – Put Together All the Pieces

In this step, you have to put together all the data that you have. This means that you are actually going to lay out the sequence now. Yes, there are going to be false starts and you might feel lost as well but don't give up. This is almost like putting together a puzzle and you have to keep joining the pieces until you get the bigger picture. This will also help you in solidifying your relationship with your prospects and customers. But you need to remember that you can keep the details for later, for example, you don't have to waste time thinking about your subject lines now. All that can be done afterward. All you have to do is scribble the entire process down which until now was only on your mind. Some of the goals that you need to establish with the help of your sequence are as follows –

- Positioning yourself as one of the top leaders in the market
- Nurturing a relationship and establishing a strong foundation of trust

- Creating a picture where you are portrayed as different and unique from others in the industry
- Impart value through every word of the follow-up
- Communicate the value properly
- Educating the prospect with all the details necessary so that reaching a decision does not seem difficult

But in order to make your prospect understand your core marketing message, you might need to be a bit repetitive because prospects often don't pay enough attention.

Step 6 – Make the Plan

It's time to get the ball rolling if you are satisfied with the entire layout and the ideas that you have created so far. But there are several more things that you might need to do and this includes creating free reports and emails or doing some graphic designing. What you can do is that you can take the help of some project management application and all of these tasks will become easier.

How to Create a Manual Follow-Up System?

Step 1 – Sort Things Out

Just like the automated follow-up strategy, you need to sort out various things. For example, you need to research about the skills of a prospect and then see how you can put them to good use.

Step 2 – Edification

If this is your first time with structuring a manual follow-up strategy, then it is always good to take the help of a mentor who has already gone through all of this and is aware of any obstacles that might crop up. For example, if you are doing the manual follow-up by meeting the prospect or the customer, then you can bring your mentor along with you so that he/she can help you boost the conversion rate. Moreover, you will get to learn from seeing him/her talking to the prospect or customer.

But you need to keep something in mind as well. If you have decided that you are going to take someone along with you when you meet your prospect, you also need to let your prospect know about that before dragging a complete stranger there. You can also solidify trust by mentioning some of the achievements of your mentor to your prospect. If you are doing the entire process on a phone-call, then you can make it a three-way call so that your mentor can join in.

Edification is the process of building a supportive network by highlighting the achievements that your team members have acquired.

Step 3 – Don't Forget What You Are Selling

You need to remember that your prospects pay attention to the part where you explain how you can solve their problems. All the other things that you say including how great the compensation plan is or the quality of your products are usually gone unnoticed. You should not be of the thought that prospects are only focused on the extra money because they are not. Yes, you can use the money in a different way. You can state the various ways in which money can solve your prospect's problems.

Step 4 – Closing the Deal

This is definitely the most important part of the entire follow-up strategy. If you are calling up the prospect then get to the point and ask them straight away somewhat like this – 'Hey, I called to know whether you got some time to review the information I gave you last time?' If they say that they have seen it, then it is time for you to make the best impression by highlighting all the positive aspects. But if they say that they haven't seen it, then it is probably because they are not much interested in your proposal. But even then, you can give it a last shot by asking the right questions and reminding the prospect about their pain points and how all of that can be resolved if they come on board with you. Remember that information is a very powerful aspect of a follow-up and you should use it wisely.

Knowing When to Stop Following Up

Is your prospect not been responding to you for quite some time? Are you confused about whether you should stop following up with them or not? Then you have come to the right place because, in this section, we discuss everything about when you should stop following up on your prospects or customers. This is also something important because you definitely do not want to waste your time on something that would not yield you any results.

This section is not about when your prospect doesn't reply for a couple of days. It's about when your prospect is not replying to you for a week! Well, for starters if a prospect is inexperienced himself or is too rude and is behaving in an insulting manner, then you should definitely consider that person in your disqualified list and not make any further contact.

But what about the others? You cannot probably mark everyone who doesn't reply as disqualified, right? Now the time for which you should follow up with a prospect depends on a lot of things. For starters, if your prospect is sharp and you have a strong feeling that it would benefit you from having him/her on board, the definitely continue following up for a longer period of time even if they are not replying. This is because you can do that much for someone you'd really like to work with or someone who is definitely cut out for this industry. But if they are not replying at all, at some point, you have to stop.

If, for example, you have sent 7-10 emails without any response at all, you clearly can see that your prospect is not interested otherwise they would have sent you at least a reply (affirmative or not). No, this is not any fixed number. You can make your decision after 5 emails as well because it is up to you how much time you want to give for pursuing a lead but 5 should be enough to make a judgment. Even if your emails are going unanswered, you should try retaining the goodwill by not being too annoying.

If you see that chasing the prospects who do not have that much potential is hampering your time and energy to chase prospects who do have the potential you are seeking, then you need to stop following up the former prospects at once. But if you have some extra time at hand, then there is no harm in putting some added effort because it is you who will be reaping the benefits later on.

Another point to keep in mind is that if your prospect is making some unrealistic demands, then too, it is kind of a deal-breaker. Unrealistic demands usually arise because the prospect is either not aware of the workings of the industry or they do not have any intention to work with you in the first place.

Chapter 9: Building an Effective Downline

When you sponsor other people through your MLM network, then those people become your downline. But what is your benefit in all this? You will be earning a certain portion of financial revenue with the help of the sales that these people, who are enlisted by you, are making. But for all of this to happen, you first need to build an effective downline. It might seem easy to you now but it takes persistent effort to find self-motivated people. So, here are 10 tips that you can follow to build an effective downline.

Finding Prospects for Your Downline

If you want to grow your commission check, you definitely need to increase your team and that starts with finding the prospects. Now you may be wondering how can you find them? Well, here's how you can do that. The first thing that you need to do is join some local network marketing groups. You also need to work on getting referrals. For this, you need to maximize the contacts that you have and also leverage your relationships to churn out the best results. Apart from this, you need to learn how you can use the tools at your disposal in the best way possible.

You can also attend expos and do a booth there. But you need to reserve your position and then plan in advance for this. You can give samples and also slip your business cards to people whom you think can be prospects. But most importantly, look at the people around you. A prospect can be anyone. All you have to do is speak with them, ask them the right questions, answer their queries, and make them interested in this new endeavor.

Engaging with Your Prospective Downline

Your next step is to use certain strategies to engage with your prospective downline. For this, you need to study the art of how you can approach prospects and what usually works best. But this does not mean that there is a standard of approach. There is no standard as such but you do have to keep in mind that you cannot let the prospect become bored or you cannot scare them off with too much jargon. You have to make your pitch engaging. Don't start off with the concept of making money. You first need to understand the person and then think about how you can land the topic of MLM in front of him/her. All of this has been described in detail in Chapter 6.

But you need to keep in mind that if you are approaching a stranger then you first need to establish a relationship as a friend before you drop in the business opportunity but at the same time don't drag on the conversation for too long before revealing your motive of building a downline.

Qualifying Your Downline to Find the Best Team Members

You also have to keep in mind that not all prospects are the same and so you need to qualify your downline if you want to build a strong team. If you blast out your request to find new prospects publicly on social media, it might bring you a lot of leads but most of them will be of no use to you. But this doesn't mean I am discouraging the practice as social media can bring you a couple of good leads as well. Building a quality downline is not just about sending out invites and then seeing who is interested. You have to choose carefully as to who should approach so that you can get some good commissions. If you want a team that's deeply rooted then three things that the members should have are enough education about the industry, a feeling of empowerment and the right level of engagement.

If your downline loses their enthusiasm quickly or doesn't know how to makes sales, then it is not going to benefit you in any way. Having a team like that is just a waste of time. Thus, you need to spend time in qualifying your downline for better results in the future.

The Importance of Service-Based Leadership

The core idea of being a leader is to maintain and sustain relationships and to direct everyone towards a progressive goal. The main aim of service-based leadership is to lead others with the motive of giving service to others. This includes shareholders, employees, and members. This approach is encouraged in case of network marketing especially because this business is all about maintaining proper and stable relationships and with the help of service-based leaderships, forming relationships becomes a natural process.

When this type of leadership is practiced, there is usually an open flow of ideas which increases the productivity levels and consequently the sales as well. Another factor that works here is that prestige is not acquired by titles or positions but by work, contribution, and performance. The common goal is met as all the employees are concentrated towards achieving it. Placing blame on others becomes unimportant and solving the problem at hand gets all the emphasis it should. Thus, energy is not wasted on processing grievances and complaints. But in order to practice this, you need to spend a considerable amount of time in knowing each person in your downline and follow through on all the commitments and promises that you had made.

"Be a Leader, Not a Boss"

What are you? A boss or a leader? This question is very important to ask yourself if you want to maintain good relationships with your prospects. If you want to be a leader, then you have to encourage your team and teach them all the skills required. But if you only encourage criticism so that you are able to protect your own interests, then you are just a boss. If you are a leader, then you will face a lot fewer challenges with your downline. A boss is a person who usually prefers to be on the sideline and not on the field. But if you want to be a leader, then you should be there with your team leading and showing them the way.

If you are a leader, then your team will be empowered and inspired and will follow you gladly. But your mission should be something that everyone should understand. You shouldn't just give them a to-do list without any context because they will not feel motivated to finish that.

Learn How to Manage Your Time

You need to learn to manage your time wisely if you want to build an effective downline. This is because you have to keep some time to mentor your downline and teach them all the tactics that you have learned through your own experience. Proper mentoring will help your downline to make more sales and this will ultimately fetch you more commission. You will have a busy schedule if you are planning to start a network marketing business and that is why you need to develop effective time management tactics to handle everything efficiently.

You have to see in which areas you are spending most of your time. Make a list and then figure out if your energy and time are being spent in the wrong areas which are not bringing you any results. And that is how you have to manage your time so that you can build a strong downline.

Stay Consistent in Your Leadership

If you do not figure out what helps you to stay consistent then you can never be a successful network marketer. You need to stay consistent with your leadership as well. If you have committed to doing something, plan it out and complete it. Stop procrastinating. One of the reasons why people procrastinate and don't embark on an activity they thought about before is because they think they are not good enough for it, which means, low self-esteem. Whenever you are in such a predicament, you need to remind yourself that no one is going to do your task for you. You have to do it yourself and so you need to get up and get the work done.

Stop setting any unreachable or unrealistic goals. You need to set goals that you can reach because when you accomplish these goals, you will automatically feel motivated to be more productive. All the mini victories on your way to your ultimate goal will boost your self-confidence and this exact thing will make you the perfect leader that your downline will look up to.

Keep the Lines of Communication Open

As you must have heard it a thousand times over, communication is the key to network marketing. The sooner you understand this, the better. You need to educate your prospects and you need to listen to all that they have to say or ask because only then can you build a good downline. Moreover, a sense of belonging is what everybody loves and you have to learn to give them that. Everyone wants to feel important and doing that will give you quite good prospects as well. One of the things that you should do is check your downline report from time to time because that will help you recognize who is active and who is not.

It is your task to communicate with all the members on a weekly basis because this will promote them to be more active. If someone is actively sponsoring new customers, then you should keep that in mind and keep your communication lines open for that person at all times. Irrespective of the active and inactive members, you should always send out a weekly message. This can be some thoughts for the week, training tips, business updated or some contest that will keep the downline working.

Encourage Your Downline to Leverage Their Strengths

Motivating your downline is very similar to posting blogs. You need to be consistent in order for it to make some impact. Always remember, for your downline, you are the upline and they draw inspiration from you. So, if you tell them how they should leverage their strengths, they will do that. You are their mentor and idol. So, the first thing that you need to do is recognize their efforts. They will feel special and more motivated to produce such results consistently. You need to remember that every signup in your business is worthy of a celebration so whenever someone in your downline brings someone in, you need to celebrate that.

You need to point out the strengths of your downline and show them how they can leverage it. For this, you can conduct some seminars or meetings where you can teach them new tactics every week. You need to understand that everyone in your downline has something special and that is different for everyone so don't set your expectations too high.

Train, Inspire and Motivate

It is imperative that you spend time and energy honing the skills of your downline. That is why 'train, inspire and motivate' should be your mantra. It might or might not be easy for you but either way, what is important is that you need to understand the importance of training. The moment you take the lead over your team you will feel a sense of joy that is quite rewarding. The success of your network marketing business relies entirely on teamwork and thus, you have to create a frenzy of excitement and enthusiasm to keep your team working.

Never forget that you are building a team and all of this is not about you but others in your team as well. You need to take your eyes off yourself and help everyone in your downline to achieve their goals. But yes, initially people in your downline might find it hard to believe that someone is actually helping them out and not presenting any clickbait. So, you need to keep your calm and go on inspiring them because there will come a time when they will understand that it is a two-way process and that making them successful will, in turn, help you achieve your ultimate goal.

Chapter 10: Handling Rejection Like A Pro

Everyone has a natural tendency to want others to like them but this does not happen at all times. Sometimes, people might not agree with you and there is nothing that you can do about it. Most network marketers take it personally whenever someone rejects their idea that they have proposed. But you need to keep in mind that whenever you want to be successful in some business no matter what business it is, you will face rejection multiple times. And thus, it is imperative that you recognize rejection being just a part of the business. The world will not come to an end if one prospect has rejected your proposal.

It is true that no one really gets comfortable being rejected. They only become a pro at handling it so that the rejection does not affect their business mindset. You have to do the same as well. It is a part of the success formula. And so here are some tips for you that will give you an insight into how you can handle rejection.

Detach from the Outcome Before You Even Start

When you become too attached to your work, it definitely plays a major role in framing your identity and all of this is definitely not a bad thing as long as all of it is positive. But when you are too dependent on the outcome emotionally and if you fail to achieve that outcome somehow, then your entire focus might break. So, to prevent that from happening, you need to detach yourself from the outcome before you start. This will take you a long way through your journey of network marketing.

You may or may not achieve all the goals that you had previously set and there is nothing wrong with that. You should not think of yourself as a complete failure just because you couldn't reach your goals but that is what most people do. But you also need to know that most people who have succeeded in the world of network marketing have missed their goals many more times than they have achieved them. But they never gave up. They learned from the mistakes they made and came up with a better plan and that is exactly what you need to do.

When you detach yourself from the outcomes, you will feel confident. You will stop feeling the need to control everything. Sometimes, things are just not in your control. So, you need to keep your faith in your abilities and go on giving your best. In the end, things will fall into place and even if they don't, you'll know that at least you tried. But all of this doesn't mean that you should not have expectations and dreams. You should have them but you should also know that failure might come to you and it is natural.

Consider Asking Why They Rejected Your Offer

You need to treat every rejection in your career in network marketing as a learning experience. These experiences are what will help you in the future to make better choices. But for that, the first step to take is to ask for clarification as to why the prospect rejected your offer. This will give you a clear reason as to how the prospect is viewing your offer and why they thought that it was not enough. In this step, you have to find out why you got rejected in the first place so that you can take the necessary steps accordingly.

One of the most common ways to ask is directly – 'If you don't mind, can you elaborate as to why you said no?' There is no harm in asking this. You could also ask what you could have done if not that. Another thing that you can ask your prospects is where do they think you can improve. When you get the responses to these questions, you need to keep them in mind. This will serve as an extremely valuable form of feedback for you. In fact, you can ask more questions if you want to. The three questions that I have mentioned here are not the only ones that you can ask.

Asking these questions is necessary because they will give you more clarity and greater the clarity, the more information you will have to move forward in the future. You might even learn a new angle or something new from the feedback given by the prospect especially if you are just a beginner. Thus, asking about why they rejected you might give you a piece of knowledge that you were not even aware of. Moreover, someone who has just rejected you will be brutally honest with you, unlike others who might be sugarcoating things.

Refrain from Investing Your Emotion into It

When you've spent maximum portions of your day into building something, rejection definitely hits hard and it is quite difficult to not get attached to something you have been doing with so much love and passion. But your prospects won't always view all of this from your eyes and they will always have their own opinions which can be harsh. They may straight away reject what you have built and proposed. And this is not only happening to you but it happens to the best of the lot as well.

Do you know what the key to handling rejection like a pro is? It is mastering the art of refraining from investing your emotions into your work. You need to stay open-minded and see the rejection as an opportunity. During this rejection, you will be introduced to several new ideas that you can incorporate only if you know how to accept rejection. You also need to understand that perfection is overrated. Try to perform your best in whatever you do instead of pursuing perfectionism. People often try to evade disapproval under the guise of being a perfectionist.

Don't ever get confused between rejection and self-worth although people tend to do this. When someone rejects your proposal, do you start thinking that they have somehow rejected you as a person? That is the kind of thinking that you need to change. Never think that someone's opinion of your project is an opinion they are inflicting after seeing you. People often face a sudden drop in their levels of positive emotion just because someone had rejected their proposal. But when you stop investing your emotions into something, you will not face these bouts of negativity every time you face rejection.

Do Not Look at Rejection as a Means to an End

Do you get completely wrecked when you face rejection? Then you need to start seeing it differently because your mindset is causing all the problems in your life. Some people think that when they are rejected, they do not have any value and that they always make bad decisions or that they are stupid. But if you consider rejection to be something like that, then that is how it is going to affect your life. The moment you start taking the positive things from the rejection, the better you will feel.

If you are going to be in network marketing for the long haul and if you are serious that you are going to do this the right way, then you need to get one thing straight – rejection is just a type of sorting mechanism. It is a segregation that is done by prospects to see who is ready and who is not. It does not mean an end. It just means that you have to correct your flaws and try harder. But if you become depressed and start thinking that it is not working for you then you will never be able to achieve success in the world of network marketing. You need to understand that everything is not about you so don't frame it to be something like that.

You also need to understand the fact that you cannot stop doing something just because you faced rejection. The more people you talk to, the more experience you will get. And in network marketing, the more the experience, the better you perform. So, if you think about it with a calm mind you will understand the number of 'No's that you are getting are actually helping you to reach that ultimate 'Yes'.

Handle Rejection with Poise, Grace, and Integrity

If you want to accept rejection gracefully, then the first thing you need to do is accept it. The first response that most marketers have is that they try to deny their rejection altogether. Some people might even try to throw the rejection at someone else. That's not how you do it. You should not indulge in self-pity or blame others for your rejection because that is not graceful and above all, that is not right.

One of the first things you should maintain as a good network marketer is your integrity and in order to do that, you need to graciously accept the fact that you have been rejected and you have to do this with proper dignity. You should not waste time thinking about the fact of whether the rejection was justified or not because that is not your work to do. What you should do is learn from the rejection and move on. This is the only way in which you can move forward and learn from your past actions.

You also need to maintain your cool and stay calm. You need to stay collected and composed. You cannot respond in an irrational, hurtful, or negative way because that is going to blotch your reputation as a network marketer. When you give a negative response to a rejection, the chances are that you are making the chances of a good outcome in the future even scarcer. The calmer you remain, the more control you will have on the situation at hand. All of this will enhance your levels of self-belief, confidence and consequently push you forward.

Make Sure You Respect Yourself

You need to keep your spirits even if you were rejected. You cannot afford to get into a cycle of self-loathing because that is exactly what will bring your downfall. You should always respect yourself because you are doing the best you can. So, what is the solution? The best way to show respect to yourself would be to engage in self-talk. The natural response that most people have is that they want to simply criticize themselves for everything that happened but that will not get you anywhere.

Don't fall into the trap of blaming and disrespecting yourself or beating up yourself just because you faced a rejection. It is never helpful to behave in this manner. What you should do is starting to engage in a way of thinking that will bring you solutions instead of pushing you into a cycle of negativity. You need to work on adjusting your approach the next time you visit a prospect and then see what difference it makes to your business. You can also try and see the entire situation from a third-person perspective. Don't make any assumptions and think about all the things that you would have said to a friend if he/she would have faced rejection in their business.

It is true that when you are rejected, your brain will prompt you to spend a lot of time finding answers to your questions. But don't overthink or don't spend too much time on something that is not going to yield you any fruitful results. All of the tips that have been mentioned in this chapter are from my own experience and I hope they help you out as well. You cannot do something similar every time and yet want to see a different result every time. So, you need to apply different strategies and see what applies to you and what doesn't. Brainstorm to find new and creative ideas every day. Risk yourself every day and present your ideas to new prospects because that is how you are going to master the art of handling rejection.

Chapter 11: Why Some People Don't Make Money?

Are you someone who is wondering why you are not making enough money with network marketing? Well, then you have come to the right place because today we are going to discuss the same thing. There is quite a high range of failure rates in this industry and this failure depends on a variety of factors. So, this chapter will give you an insight into the mistakes people make and how it hampers their business. Once you know about the mistakes, you should try and avoid them at all costs.

They Don't Have Enough Focus

Are you passionate about what you are doing? Do you really love network marketing or you simply joined because you see others doing it? Lack of focus is usually present because people are not aware of what they want and thus end up doing just about anything they see and find to be exciting. The usual answer that you will see people giving is that they want to earn more money and that is why they started network marketing. Yes, being rich and earning some extra income is definitely one of the reasons why people join network marketing but that is not the only thing that should drive you. You should have your own will otherwise your focus will always be somewhere else.

You always need to remind yourself why you started with network marketing in the first place. Everyone has his/her own reasons but remembering those reasons from time to time will help you stay grounded and also on the right track. There will be several distractions on the way but you cannot afford to go off track if you want to reach the top of the ladder.

They Do Not Have the Right Marketing Skills

You need to build your marketing skills. They will not arise out of thin air. You have to keep practicing every day with your prospects. Do you think that the best coffee in the world is available at Starbucks? Of course not! But then why do people have such a craze about them? Because they have an excellent marketing strategy which has helped them build their brand and has placed them at the highest rung of the ladder. The same thing applies to you as well. If you do not master the skills necessary for network marketing, you cannot expect the results you so dream of.

If you are just starting out, then you should check some examples of marketing that people have followed and have got good results. When you are a beginner, it is not wise to invent a strategy right from scratch because you do not have the experience to do it. So, following a plan that has already been proven to be effective will help in raising your confidence. You should also attend events and other seminars where you can gain access to the best knowledge in the market in terms of the latest strategies.

They Lack Leadership Skills

You need to be a strong leader if you want to be a network marketing pro. Some people don't understand this and they end up not making money. When you are prospecting at an early stage in your career, don't be of the mindset that you don't have to work on your leadership skills just because you do not have anyone to be a leader to right now. This is not true. Your leadership qualities should be visible right from Day One. These qualities will help you in attracting the right prospects.

One of the things that you have to work on if you want to be a good leader is that you need to have a strong vision. What are the goals in your life? When you are envisioning something, your goals and your vision should be in proper alignment because only then can you feel motivated to be a leader to others. You also need to possess the quality necessary to articulate your vision. You need to be an excellent storyteller. Practice this with someone you know before saying that to a prospect. You also need to set an example to your downline if you want to lead them properly. That is why you need to be an excellent marketer yourself.

They Did Not Have Enough Preparation

This is another of the biggest reasons why people are not able to achieve the success they dreamt of. Beginners don't often have enough preparation that is required for them to walk on the path of network marketing. When people come to know about network marketing, they only think about starting. They are so excited that they don't care about any form of training or knowledge in this field before simply jumping in. But what they don't understand that MLM involves a lot of things that they are simply not aware of.

If you want to excel in the business of network marketing, committing enough time for training is very important. Yes, you have heard me right. You need to learn how you can run a home business and you also need to learn about other aspects of the system itself. For example, if you are going to talk to a prospect for the first time, you need to understand all the things you have to say and you also need to know the things that you have to say. People keep complaining that they are not making from network marketing but what they do not realize is that they did not have enough knowledge to make money in the first place. You need to be ready to commit your time to learn first and then execute it in the real field.

They Are Spending Too Much Time on the Wrong Activities

I have people complaining that network marketing is not fetching them the money they were promised before. But have you taken some time from your daily schedule to do anything about it? Most of the time, this answer is no. People are not ready to put the effort but they want to reap the results. How can you even expect this to happen? If some activity that you are spending time every day is not contributing to anything related to your income, then spending time on that activity is a complete waste.

One example of a non-income producing activity is scrolling through Facebook endlessly. This is one of the most addictive things to do but you also need to remember that doing social media for business purposes is different but doing it just for the sake of passing your time will bring your company down. On the other hand, if you spend more time talking to others who have been here before you or if you start making a questionnaire for your prospects, then you are doing something that is productive. You need to divide your day wisely. Promise yourself that you are going to spend 20% of your time on your own leisure time and 80% of the time on activities that will fetch you income.

They Did Not Get a Good Mentor

As I have already mentioned this before, I am saying this again, a good mentor can help you in several ways if you are starting network marketing. Your mentor can be someone who is part of your upline. When you are going through difficult times, your mentor is the one who will help you in navigating through those times. He/she will help you in making the necessary adjustments. But you also need to choose your mentor after great thought. You should not simply choose someone just because you are comfortable with them. Your mentor should have a history of success is his/her career in network marketing as well.

You should also see other things, for example, if you are facing some major obstacles then you should find a mentor who has faced the same obstacles because this will ensure that you get the right advice. Since a mentor is a person from whom you are going to seek some valuable feedback, make sure your mentor is genuinely interested in seeing you succeed. A bad mentor can definitely lead to the downfall of your business.

They Did Not Have Good People Skills

Network marketing is all about interacting with others and so you need to brush up on your people skills as well. You need to be confident when you speak and you should be the one leading the conversation. Even if your prospect is someone who is quite intelligent, you should never feel intimidated. Your people skills are something that determines whether you will be able to close the deal or not. The first place where your people skills will be testes is the first time you meet a prospect because that is where you need to communicate your ideas in the best way possible so that your prospect is convinced to say yes.

If you are thinking that developing your people skills is something that will take you forever or will be too tough then you are wrong. All you need to do is accept that you are not perfect and that you need to work to improve your skills and half the task will be done already. The first step is to listen with intent and then talk.

You should have a genuine interest in the person you are talking to. Only then will that person feel that you want them to do good and that is why you are suggesting them something that will help them make profits.

They Did Not Go Out of Their Comfort Zone

If you are just a beginner in network marketing, then coming out of your comfort zone is something that you will definitely have to do. You will have to learn things that you probably didn't hear before and then you have to master those skills as well. Like every other thing that you do for the first time, climbing the ladder of success in MLM will also require you to go out of your comfort zone. This can definitely be difficult and challenging but this is also something that differentiates between failure and success. If you want to grow, both financially and personally, learning to move out of your comfort zone is imperative.

Going out of your comfort zone means pursuing those things that make you feel uneasy or uncomfortable but are also important for your success. But when you have done those things, the next time would be so much easier. This is because the boundaries of your comfort zone have now increased. The moment you step out of your comfort zone, you are taking a step towards your success.

They Were Too Concerned About Themselves

Yes, you need to be concerned about how you are doing but your network marketing business is not only about you. It involves others as well. If you want to achieve your goals and make your dreams come true, then you also need to learn to help others in your team reach their goals. You need to take your eyes off yourself but not your goals. You need to get one thing in your mind. When you are helping the people in your downline, you are actually helping yourself. This is because when you train them to bring in more prospects, it will increase your commissions.

They Let Negative Influences Affect Them

Another common reason why people fail in their network marketing endeavor is because they let the negative influences cloud their minds. If anyone in your circle, be it your family or your associates, have any negative influence on you then you need to deal with that before it ruins you completely. You need to try and distance yourself from all those kinds of negativity in your life. A very important part of being successful is maintaining the positive attitude that you have towards life. But whenever you come in exposure to negative people, negative will beget negative. But I am not saying that you will not see them ever again. You can meet them only when you have to and not in other places.

Conclusion

Thank you for making it through to the end of *Network and Multi-Level Marketing Pro: The Best Network/Multilevel Marketer Guide for Building a Successful MLM Business on Social Media with Facebook! Learn the Secrets That the Leaders Use Today!* let's hope it was informative and able to provide you with all of the tools you need to achieve your goals whatever they may be.

If you want to succeed in a venture, you need to be persistent and focused and the same goes for network marketing. This book deals with all the basics you need to know about MLM and I have tried to make it comprehensive so that reading this one book will give you an overall idea about what lies ahead. You need to practice perseverance and you also need to maintain a proper attitude towards your business above everything else. You also need to have a learning mentality because without that you will never be able to achieve success.

You have to fuel your efforts with your dream or your ultimate goal. If you do not have the right amount of motivation, then moving past all the barriers and struggles that will come your way can become difficult. Every chapter in this book aims to address the common things faced by a beginner in the world of network marketing. I tried to answer all the questions that might crop up in your mind. Since this is a person-to-person business, working on having the right attitude should be your first priority. Be confident and always believe that you can do it.

Finally, if you found this book useful in any way, an honest review is always appreciated!

www.ingramcontent.com/pod-product-compliance
Lightning Source LLC
Chambersburg PA
CBHW031905200326
41597CB00012B/540